Inspired by true events if you ask my family, a complete work of fiction if you ask my son.

To my wife and children, thank you for the love and inspiration.

First published in Scotland, UK in 2020 by PMGJ Storybooks Ltd, and under licence by Brown Dog Books.
ISBN; 978-1-83952-227-7
Text © 2019 Paul Walsh
Illustrations © 2020 Graeme Young

"School done, feeling fine, get changed, DINNER TIME!"

Jay sang as he ran around his house, excited to learn what was cooking in the kitchen that day...

"Well then, what day is it, Jay?" Mother asked.

"Oh no!" He winced, "It's Friday!"

But why would Jay be so upset that it was Friday?

After all, the weekend had now arrived and he had many exciting plans in store!

"Friday dinner means one thing," exclaimed Jay,

"and I'M NOT EATING IT!"

Just as Jay had stomped his feet, his Father walked into the house after a hard days work...

"Hello Famiiilllyyy" he said.

"And what's all this commotion I can hear? But more importantly, tell me it's my favourite day of the week!"

"Yeeeeessss!" Shouted Mother & little Caitlyn from the top of their voices.

All of a sudden the house went eerily quiet. Father looked at Jay, then Caitlyn, then Mother...

"Are you ready? Are you steady? Are you... hungry?"

Jay looked at his Father, knowing what was about to happen and put his hands over his eyes, peeking out ever so slightly.

Father stood upon the kitchen chair, wibbling and wobbling as he rose...

And then, from the **TOP** of his voice, as loud as he possibly could, started to sing…

"Do you like fash?…
Do you like chaps?…
Do you like baaanz? Fash, Chaps n' Baaanz!

Do you like fash?
Do you like chaps?
Do you like baaanz? Fash, Chaps n' Baaanz!"

All of a sudden, Caitlyn joined in and started singing!

And after a couple more verses, Mother joined Father by singing and dancing along too!

It was infectious!

"That's a rubbish song!" Yelled Jay, but a little smile did appear on his face.

Once everything had calmed down the family finally sat down to eat their dinner, when a knock was heard at the door...

"My name is Snazzy Lady. I couldn't help but over hear the most fabulous song I have ever heard as I walked past your house... what was it?"

The family all looked at each other in surprise, did she mean 'Fash, Chaps n' Banz'?

"I'm sorry you must have the wrong house, Snazzy Lady" said Father.

"No! I'm certain it was here, something to do with cash, baps & fanz!"

"You see, I work for a record company and we want you to record this song! IT'S A HIT!"

The family were absolutely flabbergasted!

"We'll see you tomorrow, bright and early in the music studio!" Said Snazzy Lady.

The next day, the Family made their way down to **'Rocking Road Recordings'** to sing their song, everyone was extremely excited!

They had all dressed up as rock stars, so they didn't look out of place...

FCB

"Hey, Dudes!" said Snazzy Lady…
*"**Lets record some awesome music!"**

Father played the drums & Jay, the piano!
Caitlyn the maraca's and Mother, the guitar!

The family were in the studio, **ALL DAY LONG**
and at the end, had their brand new song all
ready for the radio.

Just as the family were about to leave, the
Snazzy lady said…

*"**Perhaps I should have asked this at the start,
but what actually is Fash, Chaps and Banz?"**

The family all looked at each other and started rolling around laughing.

"What do you mean?" Father said.

"Jay, why don't you tell Snazzy Lady the secret meaning, since you just love it sooooo much…"

Jay rolled his eyes and whispered into Snazzy Lady's ear… **"It really means fish, chips & beans!"**

"Fish, chips & beans? Oh how delightful, I LOVE, LOVE, LOVE fish, chips & beans!"

Now that the day was over, the family said their goodbyes to Snazzy Lady and got into their car.

The End